THE GIRL O

: This is a quick read summary based on the novel
"The Girl on the Train" by Paula Hawkins

NOTE TO READERS:

This is a Summary & Analysis of The Girl on the Train A Novel, by Paula Hawkins. You are encouraged to buy the full version.

Table of Contents

Introduction

It is just a daily train ride, a little imagination running wild as she enjoys the scenery from her window seat. It is something we all do, right? Rachel Watson makes up innocent stories about the people she sees. For Rachel it is comforting, something steadfast in her crumbling world. She rides the train every morning like she always has, but without the purpose she once had. Her failed marriage and her descent into alcoholism make her an outcast. She rides into town to a job she no longer has, only to come back at the end of the day to a roommate she is lying to. She has no purpose and nothing seems to be changing until she witnesses something important.

Rachel's favorite imaginary couple that she peers at every day from the train seem to be having trouble. She calls them "Jason" and "Jess". Rachel can't quite figure out where she fits in. She was wandering around in a drunken stupor the night "jess" disappears. Rachel starts trying to regain her memories from that night. She tries to piece together the memories of that hazy night.

Rachel's new found hobby is a welcome distraction from her life and problems. She has been dealing not only with an ex-husband, but his new wife as well. Once his mistress, Anna is now having Tom's baby. Rachel feels inadequate as a result of her infertility and her alcohol problems, blaming herself for the demise of her marriage.

Rachel starts out trying to offer a little information into what might have happened to "Jess", but she becomes obsessed with the case and the people in it. Rachel tries to fill a void with strangers and a case that, supposedly, has nothing to do with her. As Rachel learns to trust herself and her instincts she comes face to face with something she never expected.

Book Review

The Girl on the Train, by Paula Hawkins brings mystery to the life of Rachel Watson, who could very well be any one of us. This is what makes this book so appealing, the humanity of the characters. Hawkins manages to create an exciting story line using characters that the general public can relate too.

While murder may not resonate with most people's daily lives, the underlying problems of the characters are those that can be well understood. Most people know an alcoholic or someone with a cheating spouse. Hawkins not only brings these characters to life, but presents those in a way that makes the reader can find a way to sympathize with each one of them at some point during the story. The reader can easily put themselves in their shoes. Hawkins' characters represent the general public with problems echoing those of the reader.

Hawkins then takes these characters through a well woven web of deceit and self-doubt. The mystery unwinds slowly enough to savor and fast enough to keep the reader interested. The characters are introduced by chapters depicting their names and the reader gets to know them each a little at a time and piece the story together themselves. The layout is enticing and unique.

The Girl on the Train presents characters we start to care about and feel for. The mystery gives the excitement one hopes to find in a book of this genre while still appealing to the reader's humanity. The characters are not who they seem and even the good guys have flaws. The book leaves one thinking about the characters and their lives long after the book is back on the shelf.

Setting

The Girl on the Train takes place in and around London. There is inner city life contrasted with the suburbs and all the types of people that go with these locals. The train is the machine that connects them. Allowing people to commute from smaller areas to the big city is a common system in many places.

In the beginning Rachel talks about trying to fill the long summer days. Children are out enjoying the long days while she feels exposed and anticipates nightfall so she can hide her alcoholism in the darkness. She is already pushed further to the outskirts of her life by having to take up residence in the little town of Ashbury.

Rachel, Megan and Anna at one point all long for something they lost or left behind. They are all inhabitants of the suburban lifestyle at some point and it affects each of them differently. They reside in a town called Whitney at some point in the story. The houses, parks and sidewalks are full of growing families in the suburbs. The city is full of coffee shops, and pubs. The train is what connects the outskirts with the big city as well as the link that provides the answer to the mystery of the story.

Analysis

Rachel rides the train into London every morning. She has had this routine for a long time, it represents stability even after her job is long gone. It may very well be the only thing holding her together after her divorce and her increased drinking problems. The train gives Rachel a way out of where she is forced to live with her old college friend in a little town with no prospects for improvement.

The train is also what brings her back to her new existence at the end of the day, in the morning it brings hope of a new life, in the evening it brings her back to her hell. The train is different things at different times just like the characters.

Rachel was an ecstatic young wife ready to impart on her journey with her husband Tom. The perfect house, the perfect husband and a job in London, Rachel had it all and dared to think she could continue in this storyline like all the other suburbanites. Infertility was the first road bump, or so she thought. The heartbreak of her failure to conceive pushed her further into her relationship with alcohol and eventually causing her downfall. This is what we are led to believe, however, and what she thinks about herself. Her husband has deceived her, however, and succeeded in making her blame herself for everything. His violent nature, unknown to Rachel was hidden underneath her alcoholism. He used her weakness to hide his own betrayal.

Tom eventually marries his mistress, Anna, and they have a child together. Rachel can see them from the train living the life she had longed for. Megan and Scott move in a few doors down after Rachel has already moved out. These new neighbors, unknown to Rachel, become a figment of her imagination as she only sees them from afar as the train rolls by. She names them "Jason" and "Jess" and clings to their ideal life in her head as a means of stability. Her world is shattered again, however, when she sees "Jess", kiss another man.

Rachel throws herself into solving the mystery of the disappearance of "Jess" who turns out to be Megan Hipwell. She is swept up into an investigation that becomes an obsession. The only reason the police even question her in the first place is because she was sighted on their street the night of Megan's disappearance.

Rachel uses the criminal investigation to escape from her own problems and thinks it is the answer to help her stop drinking. She tries to keep a clear head to "help" the police and Megan's husband Scott. She doesn't realize this is just another addiction that she can't get free from. She is lacking in self-control and discipline.

Scott Hipwell, Megan's husband is seen by Megan as a kind caring husband. She blames herself for anything that goes wrong in their marriage. Her tainted past contributes to the lack of self-esteem and a constant restlessness and need to change. She can't settle on a job other than her art gallery and her drug of choice is sleeping around with men other than her husband. Her past relationships and loss of her brother and daughter at a young age leave her with the understanding that everything is fleeting. Scott's controlling personality seeps through the words little by little. It takes a while to decipher his true self. In the end it is still questionable as to his true personality as some of his actions can be contributed to his difficult circumstances. The characters don't so much change, as new sides to them are introduced throughout the book.

The reality of confused identity is in all of us. All people get up and face life day to day and change throughout molding to the circumstances that come about. All people are differ depending on the perspective of the person observing them. This book is about change, and the lies not only told by others but the ones we tell ourselves to make the pain of life more bearable.

Lastly, Hawkins clearly identifies the warped view people may be coerced into believing in abusive relationships and the damage it can do when left to permeate the very depths of our being.

Story Plot and Analysis

The Girl on the train follows the daily life of Rachel Watson in a diary form, as well as two other women. The mystery of the story is immediately notated in the early comments before the first chapter. What seems like an ordinary pile of clothes thrown away on the train tracks seems to mean a little something more than an accident, and the indication that someone is dying adds to the suspense.

Rachel's daily train trips lead to her imagination running wild with everything she sees as the train rolls by open fields and neighborhoods. When a specific house she likes to watch becomes the center of an investigation concerning a missing girl, Rachel thinks she knows what happened. Unfortunately, her alcohol problem leads investigators to label her unreliable as a witness. Rachel won't stay out of the way, however. She continues to find clues as she remembers a little bit at a time her own actions of the night the girl disappeared.

Rachel saw something else important, but can't remember. The story continues as each diary entry follows the life of a different girl that ends up involved in the case. The diary entries go back and forth over different time periods, leaving the reader to put the clues together along with Rachel.

Hawkins provides a well-articulated mystery and suspense story from unique perspective. Rachel, Megan and Anna are all intertwined in a way the reader never expects. They all have more in common than is first believed, as well.

The divorced alcoholic with her life falling apart could be a story on its own, but her life takes on a whole new interest when the crime takes place and the reader gets to go along for the ride. The Girl on the Train brings characters' lives to light separately and then together at the end when the mystery is solved.

Main Characters

Rachel Watson-the center of the story, Tom's ex wife

Tom Watson- Rachel's ex-husband

Anna Watson- Tom's new wife and former mistress

Scott Hipwell- "Jason"- Megan's husband

Megan Hipwell-"Jess"-Scott's wife

Cathy-Rachel's flatmate, old college acquaintance,

Dr. Kamal Abdic- Megan's therapist

Inspector Gaskill- an investigator working on the case of Megan Hipwell

Detective Sergeant Riley- an investigator working on the case of Megan Hipwell

Secondary Characters

Damien- Cathy's boyfriend

Evie Watson- Tom and Anna's daughter

Andy (The red haired man) - a man on the train that talks to Rachel

Tara- Megan's friend

Martin Miles- Rachel's ex-boss

Craig McKenzie (Mac)-Megan's ex-boyfriend from her youth

Elizabeth (Libby) - Megan and Mac's daughter

Chapter 1-Rachel

There is something on the side of the train tracks, something not uncommon in urban areas. There are always shoes or random articles of clothing on the streets, traces of someone's life. There are clothes jumbled together in a pile. The girl on the train, the namesake of this chapter and others to come, notices every detail on the mundane trip to and from London every day.

She admits to drinking on the way home on a Friday evening. Her choice of drink and the quantity immediately tip the reader off to a problem even before the chapter forwards to Monday morning and she is still indulging her alcoholic tendencies. She is likeable at this point, however. She is so human. This could be any of us caught in a bad situation, drinking to escape.

The detail she gives to the scenery she passes on the train everyday might not seem out of the ordinary. The same ride everyday might get a little boring. Some might read the paper, others might listen to music. Soon, it is noticed that Rachel puts her interest into details of the landscape.

Rachel admits to her own imagination running wild, she knows it is out of the ordinary, or at least other people seem to think so. The reader can chose here to take her side or think she is a bit crazy. This part appeals to natural human curiosity. It is written to do this, to draw the reader in. The clothes on the track, the people in the houses are meant to peak our imagination and set the stage for the mystery we are about to explore.

Glimpses of Rachel's past life are ever so slightly put into this chapter. Happy pictures of a time someone named Tom. The whole story does not unfold yet. The little peek at her past serves the same purpose as all the hints laid out in the first chapter, to make the reader want to continue.

Rachel mentions the clothes disappearing from sight as the train moves forward, forgotten by most like so many other things we see every day. They were meant to be forgotten, or not noticed at all. This is apparent, they weren't meant to be seen, or found. This girl, Rachel, which supposedly reads too much into things is the key.

Later in the chapter, Rachel's alcohol problems become clear and her depressed mental state become clear. The long summer days have the opposite effect on Rachel than most. She wants to hide away, not be seen. She wants to be under the cloak of darkness so no one can see her drinking problem, safe from the world. Her world has shattered and she cannot face the daylight. She struggles through the weekend, clinging to her Monday through Friday train commute to keep some stability and routine in her life. The charade is as much for her as it is for those who know her, primarily her roommate Cathy.

She calls the people in the houses by name, those she sees from the train. She's telling about their lives like she knows them. She makes the reader want to know them too. Jess and Jason, the ideal couple she imagines from afar, and Anna. A glimpse of Anna is mentioned and the impending birth of her child is perceived.

By the end of the chapter, it's clear that Jason and Jess are imaginary names for the people Rachel watches from a difference. She is clinging anything that seems normal and ideal in a world that has come crashing down around her. She admits to living on the same street as the couple before they moved in. Her alcoholic nature contributes to her demise and leaves her divorced and living with an old acquaintance at the mercy of Cathy's kindness and pity.

The picture of Rachel by the time the end of the chapter is reached is of a girl in failing physical and mental well-being. She is trying to keep up her appearance of normalcy and is only deceiving herself. Everyone else can see the unwinding of her psyche. She contributes to her own situation by calling her ex-husband at strange hours and drinking on the train, even in the mornings. Her roommate is somewhat fooled as she doesn't realize how bad the situation really is.

The mention of the clothes at the beginning of the chapter is interrupted to give a more detailed picture of Rachel and then mentioned in their decaying state at the end. They are losing something too, their validity and importance. They represent something lost and unknown, something slowly being forgotten, like Rachel.

CHAPTER 2- MEGAN

A bit mysterious, this chapter is labeled with the name of a new character, Megan. Megan listens to the trains as they go buy and daydreams about the passengers, the way Rachel dreams about the inhabitants of the house. This chapter starts explore the idea of escape. Rachel and Megan both try to escape the here and now.

Megan's longing for her past life is apparent as she focuses on her past in a dreamlike state and seems to wake reluctantly to the present. She warms up to the day as her husband Scott welcomes her smiling. Yet her thoughts keep returning to the past of what was and what could have been, especially concerning her brother, Ben. Her brother died in an accident when they were teenagers. They had plans to travel the world together. Her husband thinks she should talk to a therapist and she agrees to go, regardless of her belief in finding some resolve talking to a stranger. She talks to the therapist easier than she expects too, but her wandering eye can't help but notice his good looks and mesmerizing accent. She has become completely self-destructive concerning her own personal choices with men and her marriage.

Megan is all over the place in her thoughts and feelings, she can't sleep and can't calm down. She doesn't settle well in to a life most might be envious of. She has a husband who loves her and a nice house in the suburbs. She is reeling from the loss of her art gallery and takes a job helping to care for her neighbor's baby. She ends up quitting on a whim one day feeling dislike for the job and the ridiculousness of being there with the parents always hovering around. The parents are Tom and Anna. Megan's curiosity of their family was piqued by a screaming match she witnessed in their garden one afternoon involving two women and a crying baby. The curiosity is not satisfied at this point in the book, and never by Megan, who finds Anna boring.

Neither Tom nor Anna seem too concerned about Megan quitting and bid accept her lie without question when she mentions having a new job.

CHAPTER 3- RACHEL

Rachel's drinking problem becomes more apparent, alcohol is running her life and she is completely dependent. She daydreams about the ideal life she had with Tom.

Rachel is back on the train watching Jason and Jess. Her imaginary world clashes with her real world when she sees that her "perfect" couple doesn't really exist. The woman, "Jess", is kissing a man that clearly isn't "Jason". Hate fills Rachel as she thinks back on her own cheating spouse, Tom. She remembers finding the emails. She is angry with "Jess". Tom and Anna still live in the house Rachel shared with Tom. She tries not to look when the train reaches her old home, but she can't help it.

Rachel's discomfort increases when she runs into her old coworkers at a coffee shop. She forgoes her plan to go to the library and continues to drink throughout the day in a park.

Another empty weekend approaches, and Rachel can't get "Jason" and "Jess" out of her head. She wakes to Cathy's Saturday vacuuming and gives in to her obsession. She gets on the train to catch a glimpse of them, to see if she can find out another part of the story she watches from her train window. She drinks before she sets out her journey and makes the decision to get off the train at the stop that leads to her old neighborhood, the one where "Jason" and "Jess" now live. She has some sort of interaction with a red haired man, but her hazy state makes it difficult to tell what took place. Rachel wakes up bloody and bruised in her own bed with no recollection of what took place, and a message on her phone from Tom telling her to stay away from him and Anna. She has a sense of fear as she tries to remember the night before.

CHAPTER 4- MEGAN

This chapter finds Megan restless again and hoping for Scott to calm her down. He fails to do so, she cannot be unwound. She goes wandering has a near miss with a car. She yearns for the sound of the train to drown out everything else. She cuts her hand while out and about and lies to Scott about it. Scott responds in negative way leaving Megan more restless. The one thing she expects will stabilize her falls short. She hasn't figured out yet what she needs to recover and come back to herself.

Megan sneaks out of bed to make a phone call. It turns out to be her therapist whose voice she wants to hear. She is trying desperately to fill a void. She goes to her therapy session the next day despite her inappropriate response the night before. Dr. Abdic suggests that she keep diary. Her response to this suggestion shows her reluctance to tell anybody her secrets. Her husband really doesn't know her.

Megan's infidelity is further reinforced in this chapter and she uses sex to avoid an argument with her husband. She also begins to use her friend Tara to cover for her outings with Dr. Kamal Abdic. Her attitude towards Tara and her husband shows complete disregard for the feelings of others. She is completely self-absorbed and overwhelmed by her own inability to stabilize. She is desperate to keep he head above water as she drowns in some unknown pain.

CHAPTER 5- RACHEL

Cathy issues an eviction letter to Rachel due to the aftermath of another drunken night. This sends Rachel further into her abyss of self-doubt and confirms she really doesn't have a place in the world where she belongs anymore.

Rachel recounts her dreams of having a family and her infertility issues. She tries to figure out where everything began to go wrong with Tom. She is completely blaming herself for the end of the marriage, justifying Tom's disgust with her, as well as Cathy's.

Rachel discovers the real name of her imaginary character "Jess", Megan Hipwell. This chapter starts to bring together some of the questions of where these different characters fall into place. Rachel's shock at the news headline of the missing woman sends her absentmindedly into traffic and then to the emergency room for stitches. The doctors concern confirms that her previous injuries were fairly new and possibly caused by assault with a serrated object.

Cathy comes to the hospital to pick Rachel up at the request of the doctor and, much to her surprise, finds her sober.

CHAPTER 6- MEGAN

Megan is feeling comforted by being home with Scott and for a brief moment wants to stop running and searching. Then she leaves the house for her therapy appointment and her view changes again. Her temporary calm quickly passes, and the restlessness returns. She wants to hold on to the stability of her marriage and be happy in her situation, but she can't find a way to adhere to those standards.

Megan talks to Kamal about her past relationships and goes home to search an old boyfriend on the computer. Scott sees her browser history and a fight ensues. There are indications that Scott has a violent side. Megan mentions his possessive and controlling nature, much to the disapproval of Kamal. She says she doesn't mind so it's not abuse.

Her affair continues and the man tries to end it. She likes the power she has over the man involved. Yet, afterwards she feels like she is being watched, and can't seem to figure out the displacement she feels. The chapter ends with her wanting Scott to come home.

CHAPTER 7- RACHEL

Rachel continues to try to unravel the events of Saturday night. She can't remember what she did to scare Tom's new wife Anna, as mentioned on her phone message. She has no idea how she became injured. Meanwhile, the details of Megan Hipwell's disappearance are broadcast in the news. Rachel is keeping close tabs on the new information. She starts the process of trying to figure out what happened and how to share the information of the man she saw kissing Megan. She starts to refrain from drinking. The new addiction is the murder investigation. She wants to feel important and needed.

Flashes of fearful events start to invade Rachel's thought process. They are still isolated and fragmented, far from a full memory. Her memories are strongly related to feelings of fear or kindness. The pictures elude her, but the feelings come forward and give her clues as to what happened to her the night of Megan's disappearance.

The police are waiting for her when she gets home to question her about that night. She was seen on the street of Megan Hipwell. Anna is a witness. She tells some partial truths and lies to appease the officers. She can't remember. She lies to avoid facing the reality.

Rachel finally goes to the police station to explain about the man she saw with Megan. The police, especially Detective Riley are more critical of than interested in her sighting, but they do have her identify a suspect. She is deemed an unreliable witness due to her addiction and unstable mental state, however.

Rachel's inability to have children is emphasized and considered a defining point in her relationship with Tom. Her sadness permeated the relationship, leading to her heavy drinking and further alienation from Tom and society as a whole.

CHAPTER 8- MEGAN

Megan continues the affair, even though the man tried to end it last time. She enjoys having the power to keep him coming back. She wishes Scott were enough to keep her happy. She loves him, but she only feels like herself when she is out with new men, taking risks. It's her own kind of addiction, her own kind of high.

She talks to her lover about running away with her on great adventures to beautiful places. He doesn't indulge her, as he is still trying to leave her and do the right thing. Scott thinks she slept well because she is making progress in therapy, he doesn't have a clue it is because she has been with someone else.

CHAPTER 9- RACHEL

Rachel continues to get herself involved in the mystery of Megan Hipwell. She seems to have found something worth staying sober for. She still knows her view of Megan form the train and that kiss with a stranger must sound crazy. Detective Gaskill at least pretends to take her seriously long enough to have her identify a picture of Kamal. She tries to stay logical and refrain from any further involvement in the case.

She continues to come up with ways to possibly find out what happened the night of the disappearance and her own injury. This coupled with a recurrence of drinking poses a risk to her logic. Following basic human curiosity and the need to know what really happened, Rachel sends emails to Tom in a drunken haze and wakes up knowing something has gone wrong. She wants to make amends for her mistakes and tries to find a way to apologize to Tom.

Somewhere along the way she sent an email to Megan's husband, Scott. She is trying to create a person that doesn't exist now. She lied about being a friend of Megan's, Scott wants to talk to her. The police have warned her to stay away from Tom and Anna. Scott lives a few doors down. Her newfound interest is playing a part in her effort to stop drinking, but is bringing a new deception into her life.

Changes are also taking place in the way Rachel views Megan. The hatred she felt at her first confirmation of marital betrayal is becoming sympathy. The characters start to change in the reader's eyes as well. We start to question who the characters really are.

CHAPTER 10- ANNA

Anna and Tom seem to have the perfect little family except for the fact it stemmed from an affair. Anna was the other woman and doesn't feel bad about it at all. She likes the power she had to seduce and conquer a married man, not unlike the power Megan feels when choosing a lover. Anna enjoys her birthday in an ideal setting with the only drawback in her eyes living in the ex-wife's house. She hates the sound of the trains and the constant threat of emails, phone calls and sightings of Rachel. Her fears are confirmed and she sees Rachel outside in the street headed to Scott's house.

CHAPTER 11- RACHEL

Rachel continues on to Scott's house and tries to sneak by her old house. She tells Scott what she told the police and identifies the photo Scott shows her.   He is angry, he obviously didn't know what was going on.   Rachel is still caught in a lie she is using for her own desire. She doesn't tell Scott she already went to the police and she doesn't tell the police she is talking to Scott. She is desperate to stay involved, drawn in by the drama and the glimmer of hope that she is important to someone and needed. Rachel is forming a false relationship with Scott, as he begins to trust her and find solace in having someone to talk to that he believes was connected to Megan. She continues to fill her life with lies and false realities.

Just as she fails to think about the consequences of her drinking, she fails to see the consequences of her impractical decision to contact Scott Hipwell. She still cannot leave him alone and rushes to his home the next day on a whim after hearing of a new arrest concerning the investigation. Scott pulls her into the house quickly before she can even knock.

CHAPTER 12- MEGAN

Megan's affair is coming to an end despite her efforts to have it continue. She tries to rekindle her relationship with Kamal during her therapy session and he resists, stating firmly his decision to end the inappropriate relationship and physical force ensues after he has to remove her hands from his body.

Megan seeks affairs to gain control and bring something into her life she is lacking. When she loses Kamal, the rejection sends her spinning back into her restless and unsatisfied state. She feels like she has no control over the situation as she cannot convince him to change his mind. She has lost not only her distraction, but the therapist she has begun to need and trust.

CHAPTER-13- RACHEL

Rachel doesn't have a decent explanation for suddenly showing up at Scott's house. Her personal need to get involved to appease her need to belong cannot be expressed. She knows she shouldn't be there. She makes an attempt to express her concern and is greeted by Scott's mother. She sees right through Rachel's feigned concern and escorts her out of the house.

Timing is not on Rachel's side, for as she stands outside the Hipwell's house, Tom and Anna. Rachel has put herself in compromising situation. Anna is shocked to see her. Sympathy for the new wife is thwarted by the fact that she was once a mistress and played a role in breaking up the marriage.

CHAPTER 14- ANNA

Dislike for Anna is confirmed when her attitude towards Rachel is revealed as she

Rachel to see them together and find out.

Anna is lost in her own thoughts about how nicely everything turned out. She has a husband and a baby and her only problem is the inability to get Rachel to go away. She feels justified in her expectations that Rachel should be out of the picture. Consequences of her affair seem to elude her.

Tom keeps Anna from calling the police about Rachel repeatedly, he seems to care what happens to her. At this point in the book his concern for her seems to be what is driving his actions. Anna feels victimized and wants the police involved. Tom leads Anna home and tries to distract her.

CHAPTER 15- RACHEL

Rachel is back to drinking has finally hit rock bottom. Her bank account comes up empty and her roommate discovers she has been pretending to go to work all this time. She has let herself continue on without making plans to regain a financially stable situation. She has used the alcohol and her illusion of importance to the case of Megan Hipwell to escape the impending reality of her situation.

The evidence against Kamal is found to be insufficient. He cannot be arrested in association with the disappearance of Megan. Insufficiency runs through this chapter. The bank account has insufficient funds and the police have insufficient evidence. Rachel has no reason to go on, she feels lost. Her own memory is insufficient, stolen by the alcohol.

Her drunkenness is still leading to phone calls she can't remember making. Rachel has given up and turns to her mother for financial help. Even after finding herself at the bottom of the barrel, Rachel can't help herself when she happens to see Scott on the street. Grasping onto her last chance to mean something to the case, she chases after Scott. They go to his house and talk about the latest developments in the case.

Rachel and Scott talk about their marriages and he mentions the argument he has with his wife the night she disappeared. The subject is not revealed. The next day at home she sees on the news that a body has been discovered in Corly Wood. The body is believed to be that of Megan Hipwell, and Rachel realizes she has passed this place repeatedly and she was there all along. Rachel tries to make sense of it all and feels sick. She looks over all he notes and wishes she could remember that night.

Rachel looked for the red haired man at the train station, she tried to find answers. She talked to Tom. She finally asked about that night, admitted she didn't remember. He gave her a story about how Anna saw her stumbling drunk and told him about it. He told her he went out to find her and found her hurt, offered her a ride home which she refused. Something doesn't seem right, she keeps having flashes of being afraid. Tom's demeanor is defensive, he knows she doesn't remember.

Chapter 16- Megan

Megan is trying to sleep, she can't get comfortable. She is too hot, uncovered and pushed to the edge of the bed she shares with Scott. Trying to stay where he wants her instead of resting in the spare room. Scott seems almost controlling the way Megan describes him. Scott will question her if she sleeps in the guest room. It will start a fight. She can't sleep, he's making her worse by controlling her. The trains continue to remind her of getting away.

She gives up trying to sleep and thinks about how Kamal was helping her. She was starting to think less about escape and settling down with Scott more. She regrets her behavior during the last meeting with Kamal. She wants to talk to him in a therapeutic sense. She realizes she needs help to move on from her past. She is hoping that finally telling someone will make the difference she has been needing all these years.

Megan gets dressed and prepares to go see Kamal at his home. She is desperate, feeling like she has lost control of everything. This feeling has been with her a long time. Megan goes to Kamal's home completely consumed with her own pain. Kamal reluctantly lets her in and agrees to listen, as a friend.

Megan finishes her life story. She thinks it will all be better after she tells someone about Mac, her boyfriend of her late teenage years. They lived together and she became pregnant with a child they did not want. Young and irresponsible, Megan went on to have the child. Abortion was not an option as late as she found out. Yet her refusal to get prenatal care and the continuation of drinking and smoking reflected the dislike she had of the idea. When her baby girl, Libby, was born Megan loved her, however.

Unfortunately, her relationship with Mac had its ups and downs and she was not living in a place healthy for her and the baby. Mac left after one of their arguments one night, leaving Megan alone with the baby without proper heat, and a leaking roof. She tried to warm up the house with a fire that wouldn't stay lit. As a resort to warm her and Libby, she got into a warm bath. Exhausted and alone, she fell asleep with Libby in her arms. She woke, freezing cold, to find Libby lifeless in between her arm and the cold, hard, tub.

Suddenly, Megan's phone rings and she is warned by Tara that Scott has called repeatedly looking for her. Megan doesn't want to go home, she wants to be invited to stay, but Kamal doesn't give in. She kisses him and leaves. She finally frees herself of the terrible secret, but it still haunts her. She now feels more connected to the person she told. No one else knows but the two of them and Mac, wherever he may be.

CHAPTER 17- RACHEL

Rachel has agreed to meet her mother for lunch. The idea contributes to her drinking this day. She has been having nightmares. She doesn't know where this fear is coming from. She checks he messages and sees a call from Scott in the middle of the night. She thinks this is odd so soon after his wife's body has been discovered. Inappropriate behavior seems to follow the stressful nature of people's lives in this book.

Rachel meets the red haired man on the train. He sits next to her and talks to her. She can't remember the night they met, but he seems to remember her. She begins to feel afraid and jumps out of her seat, running to the other end of the train. She is seeing glimpses of the night Megan disappeared and she cannot shake the fear she feels and fist she sees coming at her in her mind.

CHAPTER 18- ANNA

Anna is sitting around the house wishing she could go out like she used to. The baby doesn't cooperate well with a shopping trip, so she just stays at home and tries to get Megan Hipwell off of her mind. She is unsettled by the closeness of it all, just a few houses down from hers.

Anna's attempts at getting someone to keep her company fail and she returns to thinking about Rachel and her appearance the night Megan disappeared. She is convinced Rachel is dangerous. She is convinced she needs to keep Rachel away to secure her family life with Tom. She feels threatened by Rachel, and perhaps her paranoia is justified considering her husband resulted from an affair. Perhaps her fear of his infidelity is seated in her own knowledge of his unfaithful nature.

CHAPTER 19- RACHEL

Rachel returns Scott's phone call which turns out to have been accidental. She makes arrangements to meet with him again. They meet at his home and she asks him some questions about Anna and the night Megan disappeared, and admits she was drinking and can't remember. Scott feels she is trying to make his situation about her and he becomes angry, breaking a chair. He confirms that the police suspect him as his wife's killer and that Kamal Abdic has shared that Megan was scared of him and mentioned his controlling abusive behavior. He goes from angry to hopeful in a bizarre emotional turn when he thinks Rachel can somehow help clear his name.

Rachel wants to keep investigating the murder and makes a therapy appointment with Kamal Abdic. She finds him different than she expected. He is easy to talk to and she finds herself telling him her problems. She tells him about the inability to remember and how she has feelings of these times that do not correspond to what people have told her.

Rachel continues to have the recurring dream where she has done something wrong and everyone is against her She wakes up thinking about the argument with Tom she once had a long time ago about the money for and IVF treatment. The fight ended in a broken picture frame, thrown across the room. Tom told her the next day all the things she had said and done while she was drunk and angry. Rachel hasn't had a drink in a few days and is starting to crave a buzz.

All the things unknown to Rachel make her feel lost, just like Megan's past made her feel lost. Megan was running from what she knew, and Rachel was running toward it.

Rachel goes out for a walk and when she looks up from her deep thoughts, she sees the headlines about Megan possibly being a child killer.

CHAPTER 20- ANNA

Anna is horrified by the headlines about Megan killing a child, mainly because her own child was under Megan's care for a while. Anna's feelings have now joined those of Rachel and Meagan as she begs for escape. Tom stands firmly to his decision about staying in the house due to financial reasons.

Anna fights with Tom about staying in the house. She begs him to ask his parents for help. He tells her they didn't approve of him leaving Rachel and he will not ask them. She feels like she is being watched in the house, the trains full of people make her uneasy. She hates them. Her memories of Megan holding her child fill her with dread.

CHAPTER 21- RACHEL

Rachel receives several phone calls from Scott. He is desperate and sounds panicky. He can't escape the reporters and police. Rachel agrees to let him come over to her house. She secretly wants to see him. Scott comes over and explains that Megan had been pregnant when she died. She hides Scott in her bedroom before Cathy can find out what is going on.

Rachel thinks like a schoolgirl as she worries about her messy room and cheap furniture. It almost seems like she wants to impress Scott, and she feels inadequate like a girl with a crush. She thinks about laying down next to him when she discovers he has fallen asleep on her bed. She, however, has a moment of clarity and wakes him to have some tea. They talk about the news and the story about Megan having a child before this one that she may have killed.

Rachel contemplates Scott's possible motives to kill Megan and though many scenarios make sense, she believes he is too shocked to have known anything about the baby before today. She releases the thought of his guilty possibility and invites him to say and rest awhile. She sleeps as well and when she awakens, he is gone.

Rachel goes to see Kamal the next day. She really doesn't come to any conclusions about his involvement in the case.

Instead, she takes solace in his therapeutic gifts. She feels better after talking to him.

Scott calls Rachel to come see him again. The body of Libby has been found. He wants to talk to someone who knew Megan. He still believes Rachel's lie. Rachel knows he is drunk and that she really doesn't know him, but she gets on the train anyway. She daydreams about her past life with Tom while on the train. She gets so wrapped up in her own thoughts that she forgets to be careful and look out for Tom, Anna, and photographers. She rationalizes the visit to Scott's house by telling herself Megan was a fraud and didn't t treat Scott well.

CHAPTER 22- MEGAN

Megan is back at Kamal's house and is telling him more about losing her child. She told him how Mac came back and found them both on the bathroom floor and how he screamed at her. She left and ran down to the beach in the rain. Mac just let her go and didn't go to help her until much later. They buried their daughter and Mac left saying he was going to meet someone. He never came back.

Megan talked about how she waited and waited for Mac to return, he never did. She thought someone would come to help her. She was all alone and very scared. She couldn't sleep, and was suffering greatly form the death of her child. She walked around the dark house and could hear Libby crying and smell her familiar smell. She felt like she was going crazy. She felt like if she left, she would be leaving her child behind.

Kamal confirms her inability to sleep considering something horrible happened when she fell asleep with her child. She was young, terrified and alone. He suggests she try to find Mac to get some closure and reassures her that he had not been responsible in his treatment of her.

Megan makes one last plea to have a relationship with Kamal. He denies her request and she leaves. On her way out she gets knocked over by someone running and cuts her hand. She all of sudden wants to get home to Scott.

Megan is free of her secret, but needs someone to cling to in her sadness. Her inability to sleep and settle down is confirmed now to have roots in a traumatic past experience.

Chapter 23- Rachel

Rachel wakes up thinking about Tom and is startled back to reality when she realizes she is in Scott's bed. He is obviously upset about what happened and she is too. They drank too much and she had convinced herself Megan was a bad person and she deserved what was coming to her. She didn't 'try to resist Scott.

While preparing to leave, Rachel notices that all of Megan's things are missing. There are no pictures of her anywhere either. She finds it odd that all of her stuff has already been cleared out and Scott allowed himself to sleep with another woman so soon.

Rachel starts to feel afraid and leaves. Anna is outside and sees her leaving Scott's house. Anna runs away back to her front door and Rachel can't quite place where she has seen Anna run that way before and something is familiar about her leggings and red T-shirt. Rachel heads back to the train station and is still thinking about the feeling of fear that she felt when she saw Anna running away from her.

CHAPTER 24- ANNA

Anna gives her account of seeing Rachel leaving Scott Hipwell's house. She talks to Tom about it and mentions a restraining order. Tom is convinced it's not necessary because she has actually been leaving them alone. Anna decides to deal with Rachel on her own and resolves to call the police if she sees Rachel again. She has lost her patience with Tom's lack of action in the matter.

CHAPTER 25- RACHEL

Tom insists on meeting with Rachel to talk to her about visiting Scott's house. Rachel can't help herself from getting all prettied up for him. He takes her to a familiar park to talk. He expresses his concern about Scott and mentions that Anna talked about them arguing a lot. Rachel doesn't admit she had a feeling that something wasn't quite right over at Scott's house.

Rachel and Tom talk a little and Tom states that Megan was somewhat afraid of Scott. He entices her by telling her she looks pretty and he cares about her and doesn't want anything bad to happen to her. He offers her a check in case she needs some money. He is telling her what she wants to hear, he wants to keep control over her. She wants to be close to him but knows she can't. She takes his hand and he makes her promise to stay away from Scott. She thinks he is jealous and is overcome with happiness thinking he still has feelings for her. Everything they had together was so perfect and real to Rachel she can't imagine that all those feelings are gone.

Rachel's nightmares are becoming more complicated. This time she sees "Jason" and "Jess". She sees a struggle and "Jason" trying to kill her. The sense of dread she has been having at times is there again. She attributes the dream to all of her new information and her talk with Tom, but she is still shaken up.

Rachel feels scared again as she rides the train, but she still can't figure out why. Rachel talks to Kamal about recovering memories and mentions an instance with Tom where he told her she had chased him with a golf club and tried to hurt him when she was drunk. She kept feeling fear when she saw the hole in the wall made from the golf club. She couldn't remember being angry the way Tom had described, but she believed him because she was drunk and couldn't remember for herself.

Anna returns to the places she went the night Megan went missing to try to jog her memory. She remembers fear, a woman getting in to the car with Tom she assumed was Anna, but she remembers a blue dress. She is certain it was Anna looking back at her and getting in Tom's car, only Anna was said to have been at home while Tom was out looking for her. Rachel gets overwhelmed looking at her old house and decides to leave.

CHAPTER 26- ANNA

Anna is feeling a little sorry for herself as a tired stay at home mom. She misses going to work and tells of how much she liked being a mistress. She admits she never really felt bad for Rachel, she just pretended to. She calls Detective Riley to report sighting Rachel out in the street staring up at the house.

Tom comes home and tries to be romantic and mentions getting away on a vacation. Anna becomes angry at this because she wants to talk about using money to move instead. She is angry that he won't listen to her concerns, and states that he always just leaves to avoid confronting anything.

Anna mentions that Rachel came back near the house, he slips up and lets it out that he saw her in person an didn't just talk to her on the phone. Ironically, Anna is starting to feel like Rachel felt when she was with Tom. He lies and says it was Rachel's idea. Anna continues to doubt Tom as she thinks about their affairs and what a good liar he is. Some things start to seem strange to her, like his stories about his parents. She had never met them and Tom says they were angry, but they were very nice to her on the phone. She has a drink and goes through Tom's laptop.

Chapter 27- Rachel

Cathy gets a job interview for Rachel and expects her to spend the day getting her paperwork ready. Rachel is ready to comply when Scott calls. He wants her to come over, she doesn't want to, but she agrees anyway.

Rachel finds Scott drinking and dirty, her better judgement tells her not to go into his house. He gives her a drink in a demanding way and tells her the DNA tests of Megan's baby were not a match to himself or Kamal. He is reeling from the news there were more men. He becomes extremely angry with Rachel, figuring out she really didn't know Megan at all.

Scott starts throwing things and physically assaults Rachel in his anger about her lies. Even as he is hurting her she thinks his anger is reasonable after what she did. Her ideas of how she should be treated are warped. He starts to insult her looks, but is calming down until he sees her appointment with Dr. Kamal Abdic on her phone. Scott then becomes increasingly violent and drags Rachel by her hair up the stairs and locks her in the spare room.

Scott comes in to find her going through his pictures and postcards. He tells her she's not worth killing and lets her go. She is terrified and he is laughing at her. She bangs on the door of Tom and Anna to no avail. She leaves a note and goes home to call the police, but not without having a drink first.

She was dismissed and scolded by Detective Riley for sticking her nose where it didn't belong, but told to make a report at the station the next day.

Rachel runs into the red haired man and he helps to clear some things up about the Saturday night in question. He confirms he helped her up when she fell on the stairs at the train station and that he saw her later and she was hurt after seeing her husband. He thought they must have fought and he saw Tom with another girl as well. He was drinking as well and he left her there at her request.

Rachel calls Tom to get his version of what happened and she is trying to fill in the blanks. If it was indeed Anna that got in the car with Tom, then the question arises of their baby that was nowhere in sight. He confirms how drunk she was and that he was driving around looking for her. He says he found her hurt in the street.

Rachel stays up most of the night scolding herself for still having feelings for Tom and trying to connect with Scott. She is being as hard on herself as everyone else. She thinks she deserves it. She finally remembers being hit that evening with car keys in a man's fist.

CHAPTER 28- ANNA

Anna is still fighting with Tom about Rachel. She thinks something is going on between her and Tom. She is threatened by the history they share. She insults Rachel's looks and mental status to make herself feel better. She heard Rachel banging on the door the day Scott hurt her and didn't answer it, trying to be protective of Evie. She not told Tom about the note and he was angry and compares her snooping and controlling actions to Rachel's past behavior.

Anna cries, Tom leaves and she is left pondering what she has become. Anna finds Tom's gym bag. This concerns her because he said he was going to the gym. She finds a cell phone in his bag and charges it up to find out what he has been up to. There are dates in the phone and she assumes he was seeing Rachel.

Tom comes home and tries to make up with Anna, she gives in and leaves the phone until morning when she discovers a woman's voice on the voice message. It is not Tom's phone, it belongs to a woman.

CHAPTER 29- RACHEL

Rachel starts to remember things differently than the stories Tom told her. She always thought she was remembering things wrong because she was drunk. She knows now she didn't swing a golf club at her husband, it was him. The fear she felt all along makes so much sense now. She contemplates calling the police and decides they wouldn't believe her anyway. She promptly heads to the train station, but she has to wait for the train.

Rachel's head is spinning with her new found knowledge. She knows it was Tom that injured her and that he was driving away with Megan.

Chapter 30- Anna

Anna throws the cell phone away over the fence. Tom comes downstairs and she lies to him about hearing something and coming down to check it out. He tells her their phone was ringing and they had missed the call. He wants her to come back to bed with him and starts kissing her.

CHAPTER 31- RACHEL

Rachel shows up at Tom and Anna's house and no one answers the doorbell. She climbs the fence and finds Anna and Evie in the back. Anna doesn't look surprised this time, but she laughs when Rachel tells her they need to leave. Tom has gone out with his army boys.

CHAPTER 32- ANNA

Anna refuses to leave with Rachel and she can't quite pay attention to what Rachel is trying to say. She is in another world after what she just found out from the phone. Rachel mentions that neither of them have ever met his army friends. Anna realizes that Tom has the gym bag with him and will notice the missing phone soon. She invites Rachel in for coffee.

Anna is still in some sort of denial even as Rachel mentions that neither of them had met his parents and that he lies about everything. She admits he had an affair with Megan. It was her voice on the phone she found in his bag. Rachel and Anna discuss more lies from Tom.

Rachel mentions Megan's pregnancy, surprising Anna who had not known. Anna hates being in the same position as Rachel, she still thinks she is so much better than Rachel. Rachel continues trying to convince Anna to leave. Anna won't let herself believe that Tom is capable of murder, and then it's too late because he is there watching them.

Chapter 33- Megan

Scott is out of town. She feels suffocated when he is there and lonely when he is gone. She knows she is pregnant now and she doesn't want to get rid of it. She wants to have the chance to love the baby. She misses Libby, and fear overcomes her. She calls Kamal to come over.

Kamal reassures her she is a different person now, not a child. He mentions she needs to decide if she wants to stay with her husband. He kisses her out on the lawn, the kiss that Rachel sees from the train.

Megan decides to get everything out in the open with Scott and Tom. Scott comes home in a bad mood and already it seems things aren't going to go well. His confession of the affairs results in the big fight before her death. Scott almost strangles her. Megan is so afraid she locks herself in the bedroom when he lets her go. She is contemplating packing and leaving but doesn't want to alarm Scott and invite more violence. She finds her hidden phone and calls Tom.

Tom doesn't answer and she is angry. She wants everyone to know now. She doesn't want any more secrets. She leaves Scott and tells him not to follow. She gets to the park and changes her mind about telling all the secrets. She could put herself and the baby in a bad situation. She also doesn't see the point of hurting Scott with all the details. She is glad Tom didn't call her back and she starts to head back home.

Tom is just coming out from the underpass when she sees him. He grabs her and puts her in the car and takes her to a private place to talk. Megan thinks she see's someone in the underpass.

Chapter 34- Rachel

Anna runs into Tom's embrace and he asks Rachel why she is there. She admits to seeing Megan get into his car and tells him she remembers him hitting her and leaving her in the underpass. Anna is still holding out hope that Rachel is wrong.

Tom tells Anna that Rachel is making things up, that she doesn't remember anything. He lies to Anna about Megan and then tells her it's true. He had an affair. Tom continues to tell of his affair and blames it on Anna and the new baby. He gets irritated and insults both Rachel and Anna, telling them how difficult they are.

Tom takes the child and refuses to hand her over to Anna, while trying to convince her that Megan didn't mean anything to him. Rachel tries to get Anna to calm down and distract him so she can call the police. She is unsuccessful, as Tom comes out and kicks her, knocking the phone out of her hand.

Anna smiles when Tom drags her back into the house. Perhaps she warned him about Rachel calling the police. Anna starts making Evie lunch and tea for everyone. Rachel tries to leave and is stopped with Tom's hand to her throat.

CHAPTER 35- MEGAN

Megan notices blood on Tom's hand after she got in the car. She mentions it and he doesn't respond. He tries to be polite to her, but his agitation is clear. He drives to Corly Wood and parks the car. Megan suggests that they get out and walk.

She tells him about the pregnancy and he mocks her about running away together. He tells her to get an abortion, he doesn't want it. He insults her and tells her she wouldn't be a good mother. This hurts her more than anything and she runs after him and pushes him.

Megan is so hurt by his uncaring demeanor towards her and the baby that she just can't let it go. He laughs at her attempts to hurt him. She keeps threatening him and he loses control and the next thing she knows is that she is hurt and can't get up. She sees something coming at her and hears Tom blaming her for his actions.

CHAPTER 36- RACHEL

Tom continues to hold Rachel hostage in the house while trying to figure out what to do. He won't let Anna leave the downstairs either. He tells more about Megan and actually blames her death on Rachel, because Rachel showed up and messed up his plans to meet with Megan at the house. He continues to insult Megan and Rachel. Tom admits to hitting Rachel to shut her up that night. Anna is still trying to appease Tom by laughing at things he says and Rachel can't figure out if she is sincere or trying to calm him. Rachel doesn't know what side Anna is on. Anna, like Rachel and Megan doesn't want to lose. She wants to be in control and get her way.

Tom admits to hitting Megan with a rock and killing her. He seems to justify it to himself somehow. Rachel tries to escape and Tom hits her over the head with a beer bottle while he is holding his daughter. Anna is trying to get Evie from him. Tom drags Rachel back into the living room and tells Anna to go upstairs. He makes it clear she should not call anyone.

At this point it seems Ann is still trying to hold on to hope that her perfect life can be salvaged somehow. She goes upstairs with Evie and Tom drags Rachel to the kitchen. Rachel feels something hit her in the head and then she feels nothing.

CHAPTER 37- ANNA

Anna is actually thinking about her life going back normal after Tom kills Rachel. She will finally be gone. Her thinking is completely irrational. She is completely delusional at this point. She puts her baby to bed while contemplating all of this.

Anna soon comes to her senses as she watches her baby sleep. She knows he is dangerous and she has to protect her daughter. She goes downstairs to find Rachel hurt, but still alive. She tries to appease Tom and make him think she will forgive him and all will work out. They have a beer together and he tells her to go back upstairs. She goes to the phone in the hallway.

CHAPTER 38-RACHEL

Rachel is still on the floor, Tom telling her that she is leaving him no choice about what to do with her. Even after all of this, Tom is blaming everyone else for his own actions. He lifts Rachel up off of the floor and continues to sling insults at her. She is crying and hopes Anna hasn't rearranged the kitchen. She accepts his kiss while she searches a drawer for a weapon.

Rachel manages to push Tom over and hurt him enough by kneeing his chin to get the keys and get out the door. He catches up with her after she slips in the mud. She gets away again but she is still trapped in the yard. When he comes at her again, she stabs him with the corkscrew she got from the kitchen drawer. She turns away and watches the train go by.

Time fast forwards and she's back on the train with other passengers listening to them as they talk about the house where everything happened. Scott's house is empty now too.

Anna called the police after all, told them it was self-defense. In the end she protected Rachel. Detective Riley still had some doubt about Rachel's but Anna's story coincided. Rachel and Anna were free to go.

Rachel's mom gave her enough money to get by for a while. The news came out with all sorts of lies Tom had told. Rachel went to visit Megan and Libby's grave. Rachel is going longer without drinking, but still has fears and nightmares after all she has been through.

Analysis of Key Character

Rachel Watson is a woman haunted by what she believes to be her own horrible mistakes. She blames herself for everything that has happened to her. She doesn't include her husband in the responsibility of their breakup. She feels she let herself feel too much about not being able to have a baby and gave in to the alcoholism because of it.

WE are presented with a mess of a person who was once completely put together. We are led to believe she is mentally unstable and physically unappealing after her years of decent into madness. Her flatmate Cathy is almost driven to evict her after numerous messes as a result of her alcohol use.

Rachel deceives herself and everyone else as she rides the train into London every day pretending to go to work, perhaps hoping for her life to magically come back together. She sees the same people every day on the train, but keeps herself more and more isolated as she becomes more focused on "Jason" and "Jess". She also sees herself as unworthy in the eyes of others around her. When she thinks other people on the train are looking at her, Rachel always assumes negativity. Even the red-haired man that was nice to her is questionable in her eyes.

Rachel clings to anyone she can find that might make her feel important. She invents herself as one of Megan's friends and begins to contact Scott. She gets excited to receive a response from him and feels she has some purpose. In the end, however, Scott sees her for who she is and his own violent demons put Rachel in a dangerous situation. Rachel escapes unharmed, but even the police lecture her on the inappropriateness in contacting Scott Hipwell.

Rachel is out of the investigation now. She is drinking again with no new reason to quit. She is still trying to fill some emptiness. She still loves Tom and does not see him for who he really is. Besides cheating on her, he used her own weaknesses to be violent and demeaning to her. It takes a long time for Rachel to gain the confidence to trust her own instincts and challenge Tom's view of her. When she does, however, her own mysteries, as well as Megan's, fall into place.

Rachel moves on to a different life, changed dramatically from the girl in the beginning of the story. She can now see clearly her weaknesses and strengths moving forward on a difficult but much clearer road.

Major Symbols

There are several major symbols in this book, one being the trains. The train is ever present, sometimes in the forefront and sometimes in the background. The three women are all mentioned in relation to the train at some point.

Rachel takes the train into London every day during the week even after she has lost her job. She passes her old neighborhood every morning. Rachel loves the train. She loved listening to the trains from her home when she was married and living in Whitney. She still finds security in her routine ride to and from London every day. To Rachel, the train ride is one small part of her past life and routine she can hold on to.

Megan lives in the neighborhood Rachel used to live in, and she has a hard time being a suburban wife. To her, the town means settling down and she has a restless spirit. The trains represent a longing to escape. Megan hears the trains and she imagines all the passengers going interesting places and it fuels her need to escape and find something that fills her desires.

Anna, having moved in with Tom after he divorced Rachel, absolutely hates the trains. She has hated them from the start.

The noise in nothing more than an annoyance. The hates them most of all because they are a part of Tom's former life with Rachel, like the house she is living in. She can't bring herself to like something that Rachel loved so much.

Even some of the secondary characters seem to revolve around or find themselves near a train or tracks. Megan's baby, Libby is buried near some old train tracks. She is left there with no one knowing about her like the clothes mentioned at the beginning of the book. Andy, the man with the red hair first appears on the train, meetings with him begin on or around the train and station.

The alcohol Rachel consumes and the investigation she gets in solved in both represent escape for her. She escapes from reality with her obsessions and addictions. For Megan, men represent her addiction, and for Anna, her life with Tom is her addiction. Anna is so far gone into hers that she almost lets Tom kill Rachel so she can continue to live in her fantasy world. She was his mistress at first. He has always been the center of her fantasy, her addiction. She pulled him into adultery with no remorse.

Motifs

Adultery and escape are major motifs that appear in The Girl on the Train. These two motifs collide together at times where adultery is used as an escape. Rachel, Anna and Megan are all affected by adulterous behavior. They all end up hurt by it in the end.

Rachel discovers the affair her husband is having with Anna. Her marriage, already showing signs of demise, is ended for good and Anna marries Tom. Rachel then further delves into her alcoholic escape pattern. She continues on in terrible shape until she takes part in the investigation of the missing girl. The investigation becomes her new escape.

Megan turns to adultery to ease her restless personality. She wants to be somewhere else, to live a more exciting life. She becomes the unfaithful wife in an attempt to ease her discomfort with suburban life and to escape from the overpowering memories of her past. Rachel's ex-husband, Tom becomes one of her affairs, as well as her therapist.

Anna is Tom's mistress and enjoys being the other woman. She participates in this adulterous relationship that helps destroy a marriage only to later be the receiver of the same pain. Tom turns to a short affair with Megan to escape his life with a new baby in which his wife is inattentive to him.

Tom's whole life turns out to have been an escape. Besides cheating on both of his wives, he lies constantly. He lies about his entire life. Rachel and Anna both later find out they really did not know who he really was.

Adultery and escape are intertwined together in a messy and hurtful mosaic of human interaction.

Themes

Lies permeate the book through all the lives of the characters. They are deceived by the people closest to them and they also lie to themselves. Rachel, Anna and Megan have lies hovering over them that completely control them.

Rachel is deceived by her husband not only by the affair he was having, but also by the lies about his life he told her. His relationship with his parents and the army were not truthfully portrayed to her. Tom also told Rachel lies about her drunken behavior. Rachel was led to believe that she had become violent and destructive during her episodes of drinking. She finally found out it was Tom who was prone to violence. Rachel shares her own dishonesty when she lies to the police, Scott and Cathy. Her entire life seems to be a lie for awhile.

Megan lied to herself for years as she pretended to be able to settle down with her husband Scott despite her painful memories of her deceased child. Scott deceived everybody by looking like the perfect husband, hiding his controlling, abusive nature. Megan lied to her husband by continuing to attend therapy with a man she was intimate with. She also deceived her husband and Anna by having an affair with Tom while working has the childcare assistant for Tom and Anna.

Anna took part in the lie Tom told Rachel by sneaking around as his mistress. Anna lies to herself by marrying Tom and thinking they could have the perfect little family despite Tom's history of infidelity. Anna finally stops deceiving herself in the end by helping Rachel at the end when Tom is trying to kill her.

The deception and lies run deep into the inner parts of the characters and the reader has to discover who the characters are as their personalities and lives develop throughout the book.

Conclusion

The Girl on the Train brings together realistic characters and the excitement of a mystery in a setting not unlike that of our everyday lives. Rachel's life changes drastically from the one she was living at the beginning of the book. She comes through the challenges that are presented to her, but not without scars that she will likely carry forever. All of the characters experience life changing events and Hawkins successfully brings the reader through their emotional journey.

38805848R00051

Made in the USA
San Bernardino, CA
12 September 2016